24 Hours

That Changed the World

LEADER GUIDE

24 Hours

That Changed the World

Book
24 Hours That Changed the World
Experience the final day in the life of Jesus Christ.
978-0-687-46555-2

Reflections
24 Hours That Changed the World: 40 Days of Reflection
Commit to 40 days of reflection based on Jesus' final day.
978-1-426-70031-6

DVD with Leader Guide
24 Hours That Changed the World: Video Journey
Walk with Adam Hamilton in Jesus' footsteps on the final day.
978-0-687-65970-8

Visit www.AdamHamilton.AbingdonPress.com for more information.

Also by Adam Hamilton

Enough
Seeing Gray in a World of
  Black and White
Christianity's Family Tree
Selling Swimsuits in the Arctic

Christianity and World Religions
Confronting the Controversies
Making Love Last a Lifetime
Unleashing the Word
Leading Beyond the Walls

ADAM HAMILTON

24 Hours
That Changed the World

LEADER GUIDE

by MARK PRICE

Abingdon Press
Nashville

24 HOURS THAT CHANGED THE WORLD:
LEADER GUIDE

Copyright © 2009 by Abingdon Press.

Scripture quotations, unless otherwise indicated, are from the New Revised Standard Version of the Bible, copyrighted © 1989 by the Division of Christian Education of the National Council of the Churches of Christ in the United States of America, and are used by permission.

Some Scripture [quotes from Psalm 88, John 19, and Genesis 22] taken from the Holy Bible, NEW INTERNATIONAL VERSION®. Copyright © 1973, 1978, 1984 by International Bible Society. All rights reserved throughout the world. Used by permission of International Bible Society.

Some Scripture [quote from Isaiah 53] from the King James or Authorized Version of the Bible.

This book is printed on acid-free, elemental chlorine-free paper.

ISBN 978-1-4267-1207-4

Line illustrations on page 64 by Ken M. Strickland

09 10 11 12 13 14 15 16 17 18—10 9 8 7 6 5 4 3 2 1

MANUFACTURED IN THE UNITED STATES OF AMERICA

Contents

How to Use
This Leader Guide

THE AIM OF THIS study, like the aim of the book and video upon which it is based, is to help you better understand the events that occurred during the last twenty-four hours of Jesus' life; to see more clearly the theological significance of Christ's suffering and death; and to reflect upon the meaning of these events for your life.

This seven-session study is made up of several components:

- the book *24 Hours That Changed the World*;
- a devotional book, *24 Hours That Changed the World: 40 Days of Reflection,* that provides forty days of reflections to accompany the book;
- a DVD, *24 Hours That Changed the World: Video Journey,* in which Adam Hamilton retraces the steps of Jesus onsite in the Holy Land, bringing the last twenty-four hours to life;
- this leader guide.

Using these components, you will lead your participants over the course of seven sessions to examine the geographical and historical setting of that day's fateful events; to reflect on Jesus' death through discussions of Scripture and other sources; and, ultimately, to help participants see themselves in the story, considering how the failures and weaknesses of all of us mirror those of a Judas or John, a Peter or Pilate.

The focal Scripture text will be Mark's account of the final hours of Jesus' life (likely the first Gospel written); but other passages, from the other Gospels, as well as from the Old Testament and the letters in the New Testament, will come into play throughout the study. The first session begins with the Last Supper, which took place on Thursday night; and the sixth session leads us through the dramatic and painful events that took place twenty-four hours later, on Good Friday. The seventh and final session focuses on the Resurrection.

Encourage everyone in your group to keep a Bible close by during the study and to bring it to each session. Mark 14 and 15 will be the place to begin reading. Participants may also find it helpful to read the parallel accounts of the last twenty-four hours of Jesus' life in the other Gospels.

24 Hours That Changed the World may be used as a stand-alone study by Sunday school classes and other small groups or as part of a congregational emphasis during the season of Lent. If you choose the latter, you will find some useful tools and helps online, at www.AdamHamilton.AbingdonPress.com.

Whether you will be leading a stand-alone study or joining other small groups in a congregational emphasis, be sure to make group members aware of all the study components: book, book of reflections, and DVD with leader guide. Participants may choose to read the book and book of reflections before or after the group session. Ideally, participants should have the opportunity to purchase copies of the books prior to your first group session. If this is not possible, introduce them to the books during your first group session and try to obtain copies prior to your second session.

An Overview

As group leader, your role will be to facilitate the group sessions using the books, this leader guide, and the accompanying DVD. Because no two groups are alike, this guide has been designed to give you flexibility and choice in tailoring the sessions for your group. You may choose one of the following format options, *or adapt these as you wish to meet the schedule and needs of your particular group.* (Note: The times indicated within parentheses are merely estimates. You may move at a faster or slower pace, making adjustments as necessary to fit your schedule.)

Basic Option: 60 minutes

Opening Prayer . . . . (2 minutes)
Biblical Foundation . . . . (3 minutes)
Video Presentation . . . . (10 minutes)
Group Discussion . . . . (25 minutes)
Wrapping Up . . . . (10 minutes)
Closing Prayer . . . . (5 minutes)

Extended Option: 90 minutes

Opening Prayer . . . . (2 minutes)
Biblical Foundation . . . . (3 minutes)
Opening Activity . . . . (10 minutes)
Video Presentation . . . . (10 minutes)
Group Discussion . . . . (20 minutes)
Book Study and Discussion . . . . (15 minutes)
Bible Study and Discussion . . . . (15 minutes)
Wrapping Up . . . . (10 minutes)
Closing Prayer . . . . (5 minutes)

While you should feel free to adapt any element in this leader guide to suit the needs and schedule of your group, take time to become familiar with the information below. Knowing the intended purpose and description of each element will help you decide which ones and what arrangement will work best in your situation.

Opening Prayer

The prayer will come from the Book of Psalms and should be read aloud at the start of the group meeting. Often the psalm will be one suggested by a particular Passion event, quoted in the Gospel text, or referred to in the book *24 Hours That Changed the World*.

Biblical Foundation

This passage is the same one that appears at the head of each chapter in the book *24 Hours That Changed the World*. Invite one of your group members to read it aloud.

Opening Activity (90-minute option)

If you follow the 90-minute schedule, each lesson plan includes an activity designed to help participants reflect on the subject (event) highlighted in the session or make a connection between it and something in their own experience.

Video Presentation and Discussion

Each session's video segment features Adam Hamilton speaking from one of the sites in Jerusalem traditionally associated with the events the Gospels record as taking place during Jesus' final 24 hours. Each segment runs about 10 minutes and serves as the basis of your group's discussion in a 60-minute schedule. In the 90-minute schedule, the video is accompanied by additional content on which more group discussions are based: the book *24 Hours That Changed the World* and related Bible passages, from both the Old and New Testaments.

Each video segment features some combination of three elements: a spoken introduction and commentary by Adam Hamilton, the author and video host of *24 Hours That Changed the World;* one or more scenes showing Adam on location in Jerusalem, near one of the sites traditionally associated with Jesus' last hours; and an excerpt from one of Adam's sermons addressing a topic relevant to the particular session. Plan to view the video segment for each session prior to your group's meeting. Make note of images, insights, or questions that occur to you and that you think may be helpful in leading discussion. In addition, you will want to consult the information provided in this section:

- **Sights:** A general summary of what viewers will see in the Holy Land portions of the videos
- **Key Insights:** A selective listing of key insights excerpted from Adam's commentaries, on-site narrations, or sermon clips
- **Questions for Discussion:** A set of questions for guiding group discussion after viewing the video

Note that the DVD includes some other useful items besides the seven sessions, including a bonus feature in which Adam Hamilton takes us to the "Judas tree" and ponders what might have happened if Judas had not taken his own life.

The questions provided here are suggestions. Keep in mind that you do not have to use all the questions provided, and you can always make up your own.

Book Study and Discussion (90-minute option)

If you follow the 90-minute schedule, this section highlights key excerpts from one of the chapters in the book *24 Hours*

That Changed the World and suggests several discussion questions for use with the group in response to those excerpts.

Bible Study and Discussion (90-minute option)

If you follow the 90-minute schedule, this section highlights key passages of Scripture related to the subject (event) highlighted in the session or referenced by the corresponding chapter in the book *24 Hours That Changed the World* and includes several discussion questions or suggestions for use with the group in response to those texts.

In Perspective

Each session concludes by your group reflecting imaginatively on one of the events in Jesus' final twenty-four hours from three perspectives: either in a *place,* inside a *character,* or in front of a piece of *art.* For instance, imagine yourself in a scene from the video segment—say, reclining around a low table in the room believed to be where Jesus ate with his disciples. Or put yourself in the sandals of someone like Judas as he turns his back on Jesus or Peter as he hears the rooster crow. Or study an impressionist's painting of Christ agonizing in the garden.

This section will include discussion prompts for entering into the subject (event) highlighted in the session from each of those three perspectives. Depending on the time you have available or the preferences of your group, you may choose to use them all or only one. In order to use the art perspective, you will either need to have a laptop with Internet access set up in your meeting room or you will need to direct participants in advance to go to the image website www.super-stock.com and look up each sessions's recommended painting by its catalog number and view it before coming to the meeting. Note that the image catalog numbers are listed in this leader guide *for viewing purposes only.* Any other usage requires permission from SuperStock, Inc.

Closing Prayer

This prayer comes from one of Paul's letters as a way to connect with his earnest witness to the suffering, death, and resurrection of Christ Jesus and his desire that the church be shaped by the proclamation of those events.

Helpful Hints

Here are a few helpful hints for preparing and leading the group sessions:

- Become familiar with the material before the group session. If possible, watch the video segment in advance.
- Choose the various components you will use during the group session, including the specific discussion questions you plan to cover.
- Secure a TV and DVD player in advance; oversee room setup.
- Begin and end on time.
- Be enthusiastic. Remember, you set the tone for the class.
- Create a climate of participation, encouraging individuals to participate as they feel comfortable.
- Communicate the importance of group discussions and group exercises.
- To stimulate group discussion, consider reviewing the key insights first and then asking participants to tell what they saw as the highlights of the video.
- If no one answers at first, do not be afraid of a little silence. Count to ten silently; then say something such as, "Would anyone like to go first?" If no one responds, venture an answer yourself. Then ask for comments and other responses.

- Model openness as you share with the group. Group members will follow your example. If you limit your sharing to a surface level, everyone else will follow suit.
- Draw out participants without asking them to share what they are unwilling to share. Make eye contact with someone and say something such as, "How about someone else?"
- Encourage multiple answers or responses before moving on.
- Ask "Why?" or "Why do you believe that?" to help continue a discussion and give it greater depth.
- Affirm others' responses with comments such as, "Great" or "Thanks" or "Good insight"—especially if this is the first time someone has spoken during the group session.
- Give everyone a chance to talk, but keep the conversation moving. Moderate to prevent a few individuals from doing all the talking.
- Monitor your own contributions. If you are doing most of the talking, back off so that you do not train the group to listen rather than speak up.
- Remember that you do not have all the answers. Your job is to keep the discussion going and encourage participation.
- Honor the time schedule. If a session is running longer than expected, get consensus from the group before continuing beyond the agreed-upon ending time.
- Consider involving group members in various aspects of the group session, such as asking for volunteers to play the DVD, read the prayers, say their own prayers, or read the Scripture.

Session 1

The Last Supper

Getting Started

Session Goals

This session is intended to help participants...
- explore the Gospels' account of Jesus' last supper with his disciples;
- understand how Jesus' last supper recalls the meaning inherent in the Passover Seder and anticipates the significance of Holy Communion;
- consider the themes of deliverance, repentance, forgiveness, and friendship that emerge from the story of the Last Supper.

Opening Prayer

To you, O LORD, I lift up my soul.
O my God, in you I trust;
    do not let me be put to shame;
    do not let my enemies exult over me....

Turn to me and be gracious to me,
    for I am lonely and afflicted.
Relieve the troubles of my heart,
    and bring me out of my distress.
Consider my affliction and my trouble,
    and forgive all my sins. (Psalm 25:1-2, 16-18)

Biblical Foundation

On the first day of Unleavened Bread, when the Passover lamb is sacrificed . . . he took a loaf of bread, and after blessing it he broke it, gave it to them, and said, "Take; this is my body." Then he took a cup, and after giving thanks he gave it to them, and all of them drank from it. He said to them, "This is my blood of the covenant, which is poured out for many. Truly I tell you, I will never again drink of the fruit of the vine until that day when I drink it new in the kingdom of God." (Mark 14:12, 22-25)

Opening Activity

Because this session focuses on the connection between the Passover meal Jesus shared with his disciples and the church's appropriation of that event in the Eucharist meal, prepare a traditional Seder plate and place it in a central place for the group to see.

Consult a reliable reference source, either in a book (*Make Your Own Passover Seder,* by Alan Abraham Kay and Jo Kay) or online (www.jewishvirtuallibrary.org), to find instructions for preparing the Seder meal ingredients and arranging the plate. Or simply locate and print color copies of a traditional Seder plate with the various foods arranged on it. Alongside the Seder plate, place on top of a white linen cloth a chalice and some bread on a plate, to represent the elements on your church's Communion table.

Help the group to make connections between the Seder and the Eucharist, recognizing that both rituals involve remembering the origins of the meals, explaining the significance of the symbolic meal ingredients, and saying why the meal is important. Ask the group to respond to this question in reference to both the Passover and the Last Supper: *Why is this night different from all other nights?*

Learning Together

Video Presentation and Discussion

Play the video segment for Session 1.
Running Time: 11:25 minutes

SIGHTS
- The traditional site of the upper room (a vaulted room built by the Crusaders in the 12th century AD)
- A facsimile of a *triclinium* (u-shaped dining table common in the Roman world of the first century AD)
- A Seder plate

KEY INSIGHTS
- Jesus specifically chose Peter and John to prepare the Passover meal.
- It is thought that the site of the upper room where Jesus shared his last meal with his disciples is the same room where 120 disciples gathered on the Day of Pentecost to witness the coming of the Holy Spirit.
- Though no one knows for certain, the room may have been the place where the disciples fled after Jesus was crucified.
- The Last Supper was likely eaten around a *triclinium.* Reconstructing the seating of the group around a *triclinium,* we see that Jesus would have been flanked on his right by John and on his left by—Judas Iscariot.

- According to Rabbi Amy Katz, the ritual Passover meal is intended to make the vital story of Israel's deliverance accessible to all those around the table.

QUESTIONS FOR DISCUSSION
- What do you think about Judas Iscariot being seated right beside Jesus at the table and already determined to betray him? What does that say to you about the risks of Christian discipleship?
- In what way does your participation in the regular ritual of Holy Communion help you to recall your own experiences of deliverance?
- Talk about a time when you truly felt that sharing the Lord's Supper was both profoundly sacred and deeply joyful.

Book Study and Discussion

Ask for volunteers to read aloud, one at a time, the following excerpts from Chapter 1 of the book *24 Hours That Changed the World*. Use the questions that follow each excerpt to guide discussion.

The story of the betrayal winds its way through the rest of the Gospel accounts of the final twenty-four hours of Jesus' life. Before the night was through, Judas would betray Jesus; Peter would deny him; and the disciples would desert him, leaving Jesus utterly alone as he faced trial at the hands of his enemies.

The echoes of Jesus' prediction and of the acts of betrayal by those closest to Jesus are still discomfiting. In our own age, when church leaders have abused children, embezzled funds, and more, we realize that such betrayals are commonplace. Jesus might well have said, "All of you will betray me"; and with that realization, we must look finally at ourselves (page 22).

- How do you see yourself when you approach the altar to take Communion? What do you remember of the story of Jesus when you eat the bread and take the cup?
- In what way does your participation in the regular ritual of the Eucharist meal help you recall your own experiences of deliverance?

The Last Supper was meant to be repeated in commemoration of the new covenant, just as the Passover Seder was meant to commemorate the central sign of God's saving act in the Hebrew Bible. This meal, this new Passover, the Eucharist or Holy Communion, would be a perpetual reminder of God's love, his grace, and the sacrifice of his Son. It would be the meal by which we as Christians would remember our story. By means of it, our lives would be reshaped (page 25).

- How would you say the observance of Holy Communion defines or shapes who you are?

In the hours before Jesus would be arrested, tried, and held for crucifixion, he was with twelve men who were his companions and intimates, men with whom he had prayed, worshiped, and shared life. When he went to pray, knowing he would die, he asked those who were closest to him to pray with him.

Remember, these close companions were not perfect. They had let him down and would do so again. One would even betray him. Still, they were the best friends he had; and they were with him as he approached his darkest hour (page 28).

- If you were sitting down to what you knew to be your last meal, whom would you want sitting around the table with you?

Bible Study and Discussion

Ask for volunteers to read aloud the following passages of Scripture one at a time. Use the question that follows each passage to guide discussion.

EXODUS 12:21-28
- What do you say (or should you say) to your children when they ask what the Lord's Supper means?

JEREMIAH 31:31-34
- What are the implications of being bound to God by a covenant inscribed inwardly on our hearts rather than on stone tablets?

JOHN 15:12-17
- What does it mean to accept the bread and the cup during Communion not only as Jesus' disciples, but as his friends?

1 CORINTHIANS 11:23-32
- Why did Paul consider it so crucial that partakers of the Lord's Supper "examine" themselves first? To what extent do we do that today?

Wrapping Up

In Perspective

To conclude the session, ask group members to consider and discuss one or more of the following perspectives. For the painting, print out a color copy and display it or pass it around for the group to see.

IN THE UPPER ROOM

Imagine you are reclining at a table in the dimly lit room. Take in your surroundings. What do you see? What do you hear? What do you smell? How does the food taste? Are you near enough to touch anyone? If so, whom?

INSIDE ONE OF JESUS' DISCIPLES

Imagine you are one of Jesus' disciples, reclining around a low table—a fisherman, perhaps one of the sons of Zebedee. You have been following Jesus for some time now, and often you have not been certain of what he was doing or why he was doing it. But you have witnessed some remarkable, even miraculous, things—thousands of people fed with a couple of fish and a few loaves of bread! Now Jesus is turning toward you, offering you a piece of bread he has just blessed. What could this mean? What do you feel? What do you think?

IN FRONT OF DALI'S THE SACRAMENT OF THE LAST SUPPER

Salvador Dali was the twentieth century's most famous surrealist painter. His depiction of the Last Supper includes both dreamlike elements and precise symmetry. Study the painting. Why do think Dali chose to combine the surreal and the realistic? Consider which aspects of Jesus' story Dali wants the viewer to connect in the event of the Last Supper.

Closing Prayer

May the God of steadfastness and encouragement grant you to live in harmony with one another, in accordance with Christ Jesus, so that together you may with one voice glorify the God and Father of our Lord Jesus Christ. Amen.

(Romans 15:5-6)

Session 2

The Garden of Gethsemane

Getting Started

Session Goals

This session is intended to help participants...
- explore the Gospels' account of Jesus' anguished prayer in the garden of Gethsemane;
- examine the reasons behind Jesus' agony and how those explanations inform our understanding of Jesus' humanity and divinity in the context of the Passion;
- consider our own experiences of despair and self-doubt and our struggle to recognize and accept God's will for us in light of Jesus' experience at Gethsemane.

Opening Prayer

Out of my distress I called on the LORD;
   the LORD answered me and set me in a broad place.
With the LORD on my side I do not fear.
   What can mortals do to me?...

I shall not die, but I shall live,
    and recount the deeds of the LORD....
I was pushed hard, so that I was falling,
    but the LORD helped me.
The LORD is my strength and my might;
    he has become my salvation. (Psalm 118:5-6, 17, 13-14)

Biblical Foundation

When they had sung the hymn, they went out to the Mount of Olives.... They went to a place called Gethsemane; and he said to his disciples, "Sit here while I pray." He took with him Peter and James and John, and began to be distressed and agitated. And he said to them, "I am deeply grieved, even to death; remain here, and keep awake." And going a little farther, he threw himself on the ground and prayed that, if it were possible, the hour might pass from him. He said, "Abba, Father, for you all things are possible; remove this cup from me; yet, not what I want, but what you want." He came and found them sleeping; and he said to Peter, "Simon, are you asleep? Could you not keep awake one hour? Keep awake and pray that you may not come into the time of trial; the spirit indeed is willing, but the flesh is weak." And again he went away and prayed, saying the same words. And once more he came and found them sleeping, for their eyes were very heavy; and they did not know what to say to him. He came a third time and said to them, "Are you still sleeping and taking your rest? Enough! The hour has come; the Son of Man is betrayed into the hands of sinners. Get up, let us be going. See, my betrayer is at hand."

(Mark 14:26, 32-42)

Opening Activity

Before going up to the Mount of Olives, Jesus and his disciples sang a hymn (Mark 14:26), likely several of the "Hallel psalms." (Psalms 113–114 were sung before the Passover meal, and Psalms 115–118 were sung afterward.)

Consider reciting or singing responsively one or more of these psalms as they are arranged in a psalter, hymnal, or book of worship. If you have a United Methodist hymnal, you will find a liturgical psalter section beginning on page 735, with instructions on how to follow the call and response pattern of the psalms in worship. The Hallel psalms can be found beginning on page 834.

(Note: In the second chapter of his book *24 Hours That Changed the World,* Adam Hamilton remarks, "The psalms represent the heart and soul of the Bible, and Jesus' use of them during the last twenty-four hours of his life beckons us to become more familiar with them. A good starting point might be to read Psalm 118 in its entirety, imagining what these words may have meant to Jesus as he sang them on that agonizing night.")

Learning Together

Video Presentation and Discussion

Play the video segment for Session 2.
Running Time: 6:57 minutes

SIGHTS
- The garden of Gethsemane
- A 3000-year-old olive tree in Gethsemane
- The Church of All Nations and particularly the stars painted on the ceiling in the Church of All Nations
- The rock considered the traditional site of Jesus' prayer in Gethsemane

KEY INSIGHTS

- Approaching the Holy Land as a pilgrim allows you to place yourself in the story, to imagine yourself trying to stay awake under an olive tree, or to kneel at the very place Christ may have thrown himself on the ground in agony.
- Jesus began his public ministry by being tempted by the devil. Here in the garden, Jesus was tempted once again: "You don't have to suffer. You don't have to die. Just run!"
- The Church of All Nations was designed to take pilgrims back to that night in the garden. The interior is dark. The ceiling is full of stars. Below a large mosaic of Christ kneeling in prayer is a large rock that pilgrims can kneel before and touch.
- In both the garden of Eden and the garden of Gethsemane, the crucial question was, "God's will or not?"

QUESTIONS FOR DISCUSSION

- When have you been unable to "stay awake," pay attention, or follow through when you felt Jesus most needed you?
- What significance do you see in the fact that two of the Bible's most profound temptation stories take place in a garden?
- When in your experience of faith have you heard the whispered temptation, "Just run!"? How did you respond?
- What words would you want to pray if you were kneeling, right now, before the stone in the Church of All Nations?

Book Study and Discussion

Ask for volunteers to read aloud, one at a time, the following excerpts from Chapter 2 of the book *24 Hours That*

Changed the World. Use the question that follows each excerpt to guide discussion.

The idea that Jesus was in anguish, pleading with God, is unsettling to many Christians. For some, the scene evokes great compassion. For others, the image of Jesus asking God to take the cup of suffering from him and his seeming anxiety over the Crucifixion seems to lack nobility and courage. For still others, the image may even appear to indicate a lack of faith. They would perhaps expect Jesus to face his torture and death without agitation or fear. Interestingly, Luke reduces this story by half and seems to minimize Jesus' anguish (though a later editor seems to have added to Luke's Gospel the detail that Jesus' sweat was like drops of blood [Luke 22:44], as though attempting to address Luke's minimalist approach). John does not include the story of Jesus' anguish at all (page 37).

- How does the Gospels' portrayal of Jesus' anguish in the garden of Gethsemane inform or affect your understanding of who Jesus is?

While we speak of Jesus bearing the sins of the world on the cross, the idea is not that the Father literally covered Jesus with the world's sins. The idea is that the punishment those sins merited was voluntarily taken by Jesus on the cross (He suffered for sins he did not commit.) in order to reconcile us to God. There was no reason for the Father to turn away. This was, in fact, the greatest act of sacrificial love imaginable and part of God's own plan. God did not look away but instead looked with love and anguish at the suffering of his Son. God was grieved by it, seeing in the suffering and death of Jesus his Son's effort to draw the world to God. By watching this act, the Father joined in the suffering of the Son during those hours on the cross (page 38).

- When have you been comforted by the belief that God suffers and grieves with you even as God grieved over Jesus as he suffered on the cross?

Each of us knows what it is like to sense that God wants us to do something we do not want to do. We may feel called to take on a new ministry, to leave behind an unhealthy relationship, or to give a sacrificial gift to an organization. It may be a short-term or long-term call to the mission field, or it could be a call to serve and love others outside our comfort zone.

One of my parishioners felt called to teach the Alpha course, an introduction to Christian faith, in a federal penitentiary; but the first time she approached the security gates and barbed-wire fencing at Leavenworth Penitentiary and then entered to meet the federal prisoners, she was terrified and wanted to back out. Another parishioner felt God calling her to leave her corporate job to go into the mission field in Honduras. Another felt compelled to start a ministry to the homeless. Still another was certain God was calling him to adopt a child from foster care.

Each of these people had moments of anxiety related to answering God's call; and each ultimately prayed, as Jesus prayed, "Not what I want, but what you want." This prayer captures the essence of complete trust. It is bold enough to lay before God our desires and humble and obedient enough to reassert that we will do whatever God calls us to do, no matter the cost (pages 41–42).

- Recall a time when you experienced anxiety over responding to God's call to do something you did not want to do. How did you finally come to the point (if you did) of saying, "Not what I want, but what you want"?

Bible Study and Discussion

Ask for volunteers to read aloud the following passages of Scripture one at a time. Use the question that follows each passage to guide discussion.

JOEL 2:28–3:12
- The prophet Joel describes God's final judgment of the nations as taking place in the same area (Kidron or the Valley of Jehoshaphat) where Jesus journeyed on his way to Gethsemane and ultimately to the cross. What insights does that connection give you as you consider Jesus' agonizing over his mission in Gethsemane?

PSALM 116
- Remember that this is one of the psalms traditionally sung after the Passover meal. Imagine Jesus singing the psalm and coming to verse 13: "I will lift up the cup of salvation and call on the name of the LORD." What do you think Jesus understood this to mean for him?

LUKE 4:1-13
- What connections do you see between Jesus' three temptations in the wilderness and his three prayers at Gethsemane?

HEBREWS 5:7-9
- What insight about Jesus' Gethsemane experience does the writer of Hebrews want believers to understand?

Wrapping Up

In Perspective

To conclude the session, ask group members to consider and discuss one or more of the following perspectives. For the painting, print out a color copy and display it or pass it around for the group to see.

In an Olive Grove

Imagine yourself before an expansive, ancient olive tree, its gnarled branches casting shadows at your feet. Looking through the branches, you can just make out the wall of the Temple gleaming in the moonlight. Somewhere you can hear a voice praying. What else do you hear? What else do you see? What thoughts are running through your mind?

Inside the Heart of Judas

Imagine that you are Judas. You have just kissed your friend Jesus for the last time, and in so doing you have condemned him to death. You can see the soldiers shoving Jesus on ahead of them, out of the garden. You are alone. Your fellow disciples have fled into the night. You collapse against the trunk of the olive tree. You can see the impressions on the ground where Jesus must have been praying. What do you feel now?

In Front of Gauguin's Agony in the Garden

The French painter Paul Gauguin is probably best known for his series of primitivist studies of Tahitian life, characterized by simple but vibrant color. In his depiction of Jesus at Gethsemane, notice that the background of dark greens and blues includes several full trees and two figures dressed in black. Most striking is the vivid orange color of Jesus' hair, which immediately draws your attention to his face. Look carefully at Jesus' expression, the position of his hands, and the placement of the bare tree immediately behind him. What emotion do you think the artist is conveying? What might be the piece of paper Jesus is holding? What is the purpose of the bare tree? How does Gauguin's image of the Gethsemane story compare with your own?

Closing Prayer

Now may the God of peace, who brought back from the dead our Lord Jesus, the great shepherd of the sheep, by the blood of the eternal covenant, make you complete in everything good so that you may do his will, working among us that which is pleasing in his sight, through Jesus Christ, to whom be the glory forever and ever. Amen. (Hebrews 13:20-21)

Session 3

Condemned by the Righteous

Getting Started

Session Goals

This session is intended to help participants...
- explore the Gospels' account of Jesus' trial before the high priest Caiaphas and the Sanhedrin;
- understand some of the motivations of the Jewish officials who brought Jesus to trial in secret and during the night—in particular, to examine the roles fear, insecurity, and the need for power played in the condemnation of an innocent man by supposedly pious leaders;
- consider how this part of Jesus' story underscores the way fear can poison us into remaining silent in the face of wrongdoing and denying the truth of Christ.

Opening Prayer

O LORD, God of my salvation,
when, at night, I cry out in your presence,

let my prayer come before you;
   incline your ear to my cry.

For my soul is full of troubles,
   and my life draws near to Sheol.
I am counted among those who go down to the Pit.

(Psalm 88:1-4)

Biblical Foundation

They took Jesus to the high priest; and all the chief priests, the elders, and the scribes were assembled.... Now the chief priests and the whole council were looking for testimony against Jesus to put him to death.... The high priest asked him, "Are you the Messiah, the Son of the Blessed One?" Jesus said, "I am; and

'you will see the Son of Man

seated at the right hand of the Power,'

and 'coming with the clouds of heaven.'"

Then the high priest tore his clothes and said, "Why do we still need witnesses? You have heard his blasphemy! What is your decision?" All of them condemned him as deserving death. Some began to spit on him, to blindfold him, and to strike him, saying to him, "Prophesy!" The guards also took him over and beat him.

While Peter was below in the courtyard, one of the servant-girls of the high priest came by. When she saw Peter warming himself, she stared at him and said, "You also were with Jesus, the man from Nazareth." But he denied it, saying, "I do not know or understand what you are talking about."... After a little while the bystanders again said to Peter, "Certainly you are one of them; for you are a Galilean." But he began to curse, and he swore an oath, "I do not know this man you are talking about." At that moment the cock crowed for the second time. Then Peter remembered that Jesus had said to him, "Before the cock crows twice, you will deny me three times." And he broke down and wept.

(Mark 14:53, 55, 61-68, 70-72)

Opening Activity

Just outside Jerusalem, located on the southeastern slope of Mount Zion, stands the Church of Saint Peter in Gallicantu (which means "cock crowing"). In the courtyard is a sculpture commemorating Peter's triple denial of Christ. It features a tall column with a rooster on the top and four figures around its base: Peter is seated with his hands outstretched in a posture of utter denial and dismissal. He is flanked by a Roman guard (Mark 14:54b) and two servant girls (Mark 14:66-72; also Matthew 26:69-75—the sculpture depicts two different women in accordance with the Matthew passage, even though Mark indicates the same servant girl speaks twice). The Latin inscription on the sculpture's base (*non novi illum*) is taken from Luke 22:57: "But he denied it, saying, 'Woman, I do not know him.'"

Print out a photo of the sculpture and display it or pass it around for the group to see. Then invite group members to imagine their most egregious betrayal of another person on display as a statue. What would be its features?

Learning Together

Video Presentation and Discussion

Play the video segment for Session 3.

Running Time: 9:15 minutes

SIGHTS
- The steep stone incline leading up to Caiaphas' house
- Outside the ruins of the site believed to be the palace home of Caiaphas the high priest

- The pit discovered beneath the ruins of Caiaphas' house, likely a holding place for prisoners awaiting trial
- Inside the Church of Peter at Gallicantu
- The statue of Peter, which depicts his three denials

KEY INSIGHTS

- The walk from the garden of Gethsemane, across the Kidron Valley, and up to the high priest's home takes about twenty minutes; Jesus would have walked at night, probably barefoot.
- In antiquity, a prison was often no more than a pit or dry cistern. Jesus was likely lowered into a pit like the one found beneath the ruins of Caiaphas' house and perhaps held for five, six, or seven hours.
- While we focus on Peter denying Christ during his appearance before the Sanhedrin, we should remember that Peter was the only disciple to come to the place Jesus was to be tried.

QUESTIONS FOR DISCUSSION

- Imagine what it would have been like to walk barefoot for twenty minutes up to where you were then lowered into a pit, hands shackled above your head for several hours. What do you think Jesus may have been thinking? feeling? What would you be thinking? feeling?
- Recall the image of the statue of Peter that depicts his three denials. What aspects of Peter and his betrayal did the sculptor want the viewer to consider?
- The statement is made at the end of the video segment that "if there is hope for Peter, there is hope for us." To what extent has that been true for you in your faith experience?

Book Study and Discussion

Ask for volunteers to read aloud, one at a time, the following excerpts from Chapter 3 of the book *24 Hours That Changed the World*. Use the questions that follow each excerpt to guide discussion.

We need to step back from this scene for a moment to recognize its full import and appreciate its tragic irony. Christians believe that in Jesus, God walked in human flesh on this earth. He was in that sense like an emperor who so desires to know his subjects that he dons ordinary clothes and lives among them, with no one recognizing or understanding him. The God of the universe chose to walk in human flesh as an itinerant preacher, teacher, carpenter, healer—and pauper. He came as one of us. He healed the sick, forgave sinners, showed compassion to the lost, and taught people what God was really like. We must not miss the irony here: It was not the "sinners" who arrested God when he walked among us. Those who took him into custody and tried him were the most pious and religious people on the face of the earth. The God they claimed to serve walked among them in flesh, and they could not see him. They were so blinded by their love of power and their fear of losing it that they missed him (page 48).

- In what ways would you say Jesus is still a threat to people's way of life today?
- To what extent do you think people's resistance to Jesus and his message is motivated by fear?

No one spoke up in the Sanhedrin. No one asked, "Is this really in keeping with our faith?" How many times in recent history has the same thing happened—during the Holocaust, in Jim Crow America, in South Africa, at Abu Ghraib, and in your life and mine. How many times have we known something was wrong but were afraid to speak up? I am not talking about simply pointing out other people's sins. We all know Christians who freely point out the sins of others; they are not being courageous, just obnoxious. I am talking about those times when you are part of a group about to do something that is clearly wrong or when you see injustice being done to someone and all it would take would be one person speaking up, but everyone remains silent. What would have happened if one or two or three of those Sanhedrin members had simply said, "This isn't right, regardless of what we think about this man. It's not in keeping with what God teaches us" (page 52).

- When have you chosen to be silent rather than speak up on behalf of the truth?

Finally, they looked at Jesus; and the high priest said, "Are you the Messiah, the Son of the Blessed One?" (Mark 14:61). All Jesus had to do was to keep silent, and there would have been no grounds for conviction; instead he replied in a manner deemed blasphemous for Jews and traitorous for Romans.

Jesus' response to this question of his identity brings together three Old Testament allusions, each of which assured his conviction by the Sanhedrin. Let's consider each of these. Jesus' first statement is easy to read as a simple, literal answer to the question, "Are you the Messiah?" Mark records it as two Greek words: "Ego eimi," or "I am" (Mark 14:62). Caiaphas, though, realized this was not a simple declarative. The straightforward answer would have been, "I am he," "I am the Blessed One," or even "I am the Messiah." But a simple "I am" in the Greek seems to point toward something much more profound (page 53).

- The Greek words *Ego eimi* ("I am") contain a powerful proclamation about who Jesus is. Imagine Jesus speaking those words directly to you. What might he say to you in completing that thought: "I am _____ "?

The incident [Peter's denial] is one of the few that is mentioned in all four Gospels, so all four writers must have considered it important. It was not included in order to embarrass Peter. The Gospels were written, in fact, after (tradition tells us) Peter had been crucified upside down for his faith. The Gospel writers knew the story because Peter must have regularly told the awful truth of that episode himself. None of the other disciples (except John) was there. Peter must have told it when he went to preach. Peter would surely have said, "I know you've denied Jesus. I denied him myself. I denied him in a way that I am deeply ashamed of, and yet I have to tell you: I betrayed the Lord, but he gave me grace. He took me back. And if you've denied him, he will take you back, too." Peter wanted to reassure others that, despite the fact that there are times when all of us deny the Lord, he will continue to take us back and use us to accomplish his work. From that moment forward, Peter would never again deny Jesus (page 58).

- When have you experienced the shame of realizing that you had denied Christ and longed for the assurance of his forgiveness?

Bible Study and Discussion

Ask for volunteers to read aloud the following passages of Scripture one at a time. Use the question that follows each passage to guide discussion.

EXODUS 3:1-14

Because Jesus' suffering and death did not conform to the conventional messianic expectations of the day, the Gospel writers frequently appealed to the Old Testament to make sense of Jesus' mission and messiahship. How does the burning bush story in Exodus 3 help make sense of Jesus' response to Caiaphas in Mark 14:62?

PSALM 110:1-4

How does the allusion to Melchizedek give meaning to Jesus' role as God's Messiah?

HEBREWS 5:7-9

Reflect on the scene of Jesus' trial in light of these verses from Hebrews. How is it possible to hold to the claim that "God is love" and also hear Jesus' anguished plea, "Abba, Father...; remove this cup from me; yet, not what I want but what you want" (Mark 14:36)?

Wrapping Up

In Perspective

To conclude the session, ask group members to consider and discuss one or more of the following perspectives. For the painting, print out a color copy and display it or pass it around for the group to see.

IN THE PALACE OF CAIAPHAS

Little remains of what is believed to have been the house of Caiaphas, but excavations made after the Six-Day War in 1967 revealed the ruins of several homes (called Herodian mansions) that likely were occupied by the rich and powerful Temple priests. These remains and artifacts are now lodged at the Wohl Archaeological Museum, where they bear witness to the remarkably luxurious standard of living—mosaic floors, frescoes, valuable glassware and ceramics—enjoyed by

Jerusalem's Upper City dwellers. Imagine that you are inside the palatial home of the high priest. You stand under an ornate archway or lean against a cool stone column. A group of richly robed Jewish leaders sweeps past you, muttering among themselves. You follow them to the front gate, where a crowd is gathering. What do you hear? What do you see happening? What is the feeling in the house?

INSIDE PETER

Imagine that you are Peter, slinking about the courtyard outside the house of Caiaphas. You linger near the edges among the flickering shadows because you are trying to hear what is going on inside the house and to avoid any contact with other people at the same time. Go inside Peter's heart to sense his pain as he hears himself deny knowing Jesus. Listen with Peter's ears to what you hear happening to Jesus inside the house.

IN FRONT OF TISSOT'S CHRIST IS MOCKED IN THE HOUSE OF CAIAPHAS

Nineteenth-century French painter James Joseph Jacques Tissot was a popular portrait artist and caricaturist who, in 1886, made his first trip to Palestine and then spent the next decade researching and illustrating detailed scenes from the Bible in watercolor. This particular painting depicts a frenetic scene in which Jesus is being humiliated by a mob outside a columned entryway. Notice how Jesus' posture contrasts with those who hold him, poke him, and mock him. A young man in the bottom-left corner looks back at the viewer with a troubled expression. What is he thinking? What is his role in the painting?

Closing Prayer

Blessed be the God and Father of our Lord Jesus Christ, the Father of mercies and the God of all consolation, who consoles us in all our affliction, so that we may be able to console those who are in any affliction with the consolation with which we ourselves are consoled by God. For just as the sufferings of Christ are abundant for us, so also our consolation is abundant through Christ. Amen. (2 Corinthians 1:3-5)

Session 4

Jesus, Barabbas, and Pilate

Getting Started

Session Goals

This session is intended to help participants...
- explore the Gospels' account of Jesus' trial before Pontius Pilate;
- explore the meaning of Jesus' seeming determination to submit himself to suffering and ultimately death at the hands of religious and political authorities;
- consider how Jesus' suffering is understood to be purposeful and redemptive by examining the themes of atonement, messiahship, and the "suffering servant."

Opening Prayer

The LORD is my light and my salvation;
    whom shall I fear?
The LORD is the stronghold of my life;
    of whom shall I be afraid?

When evildoers assail me
>   to devour my flesh—
my adversaries and foes—
>   they shall stumble and fall.

Though an army encamp against me,
>   my heart shall not fear;
though war rise up against me,
>   yet I will be confident....

Teach me your way, O LORD,
>   and lead me on a level path
>   because of my enemies.
Do not give me up to the will of my adversaries,
>   for false witnesses have risen against me,
>   and they are breathing out violence.

I believe that I shall see the goodness of the LORD
>   in the land of the living.
Wait for the LORD;
>   be strong, and let your heart take courage;
>   wait for the LORD! (Psalm 27:1-3, 11-14)

Biblical Foundation

As soon as it was morning, the chief priests held a consultation with the elders and scribes and the whole council. They bound Jesus, led him away, and handed him over to Pilate. Pilate asked him, "Are you the King of the Jews?" He answered him, "You say so." Then the chief priests accused him of many things. Pilate asked him again, "Have you no answer? See how many charges they bring against you." But Jesus made no further reply, so that Pilate was amazed.

Now at the festival he used to release a prisoner for them, anyone for whom they asked. Now a man called Barabbas was in prison with the rebels who had committed murder during the insurrection. So the crowd came and began to ask Pilate to do for them according to his custom. Then he answered them, "Do you want me to release for you the King of the Jews?" For he realized that it was out of jealousy that the chief priests had handed him over. But the chief priests stirred up the crowd to have him release Barabbas for them instead. Pilate spoke to them again, "Then what do you wish me to do with the man you call the King of the Jews?" They shouted back, "Crucify him!" Pilate asked them, "Why, what evil has he done?" But they shouted all the more, "Crucify him!" So Pilate, wishing to satisfy the crowd, released Barabbas for them; and after flogging Jesus, he handed him over to be crucified. (Mark 15:1-15)

Opening Activity

Before the session begins, place on a central table a basin of water and a towel. To begin the activity, ask someone to read aloud Matthew 27:24: "So when Pilate saw that he could do nothing, but rather that a riot was beginning, he took some water and washed his hands before the crowd, saying, 'I am innocent of this man's blood; see to it yourselves.'"

As the passage is read, step up to the table and wash your hands in water from the basin; then dry them. Ask group members to recall a time when they used (or heard someone else use) the phrase, "I wash my hands of this," to deflect responsibility for some action. Reflect on how this phrase, often used glibly in reference to some relativel benign incident, has its roots in Pilate's decision to give Jesus over to be crucified without retaining any responsibility for it.

Learning Together

Video Presentation and Discussion

Play the video segment for Session 4.
Running Time: 9:10 minutes

SIGHTS

- The opening shot of a busy street—a sharp contrast to the likely empty street Jesus walked, early in the morning, from the house of Caiaphas to the Fortress Antonia, the traditional site of his trial before Pilate
- A scale model of the city of Jerusalem and the Temple as they looked in Jesus' day
- A priest leading pilgrims along the Via Dolorosa
- The stone pavement (called *lithostrotos*) where the crowd gathered for the trial before Pilate

KEY INSIGHTS

- The Via Dolorosa, or the Way of Suffering, marks the steps of Jesus from his condemnation before Pilate to his burial.
- The Stations of the Cross, developed by the Franciscans in the fourteenth century, is a devotional journey of fourteen stops, allowing pilgrims to retrace Jesus' journey along the Way of Suffering.
- Pilate gave the crowd a choice between Jesus Barabbas and his call to take up arms and Jesus of Nazareth and his call to love. The crowd chose violence.
- Imagine the sound echoing off the stone pavement, "Crucify him!"

QUESTIONS FOR DISCUSSION

- Why do you think early Christians developed devotional exercises such as the Stations of the Cross? What can you imagine feeling as you followed behind someone carrying a cross along the Via Dolorosa?

- In what ways are we still presented with the opportunity to confront our culture by choosing the way of love (Jesus) or the way of violence (Barabbas)?
- If you had been at Jesus' trial, which character would you most likely identify with: Pilate? the crowd? Barabbas?

Book Study and Discussion

Ask for volunteers to read aloud, one at a time, the following excerpts from Chapter 4 of the book *24 Hours That Changed the World*. Use the questions that follow each excerpt to guide discussion.

As he had at the trial before the Sanhedrin, Jesus remained virtually silent before Pilate, who was astounded at his unwillingness to defend himself. Pilate knew the chief priests were accusing Jesus out of envy—Jesus was becoming more popular than they were, and their fear and insecurity drove their hatred—but why, he wondered, wasn't Jesus defending himself? He was charged with claiming to be king of the Jews, a capital offense. Caesar was king of the Jews now, and claiming that title was a sign of rebellion. When Pilate asked Jesus, "Are you the King of the Jews?" (Mark 15:2a), Jesus gave a short and cryptic answer: "You say so" (Mark 15:2b). Jesus might have been saying, "Yes, of course, I am." He might have meant simply, "You have spoken, and I am not going to disagree with you." But he did not elaborate. In Matthew, Mark, and Luke, Jesus did not say another word to Pilate. And so, Pilate must have wondered, "Why isn't he speaking?" (page 63).

- Why do you think the Synoptic Gospels show Jesus choosing not to speak in defense of himself?

47

Jesus was offering himself as a sacrificial lamb for the sins of the world. His death, Christians believe, was redemptive. It was purposeful. Jesus did not die a disillusioned prophet. He was not simply a great teacher put to death by the Romans. He chose to go to Jerusalem, anticipating and even predicting to his disciples his death. Christians believe that that death was the vehicle by which God saved the world....

Theologians have long wrestled with how we are to understand the doctrine of the Atonement—that is, the at-one-ment of God and humankind, our reconciliation with God through Jesus' death on the cross. Most thoughtful people wrestle with the question. It is difficult for us to comprehend fully at first glance how the death of Jesus brings about our salvation; it is something of an enigma (page 65).

- How do you explain the connection between Jesus' suffering and the world's salvation? What about the doctrine(s) of the Atonement do you struggle to comprehend?

Matthew makes clear the crowd was being given a choice between two messianic figures. If you picture yourself as part of that crowd, which one do you pick? One is going to lead by force; throw out the Romans; reclaim your tax money, wealth, and prosperity; and restore the strength of the Jewish kingdom. The other's leadership involves loving these same oppressors, serving them as they dwell among you, doubling the service they demand of you....

Jesus asks us to choose his way over the way of Barabbas; but I also know that while many admire Jesus of Nazareth, they feel safer with, and prefer, Jesus Barabbas. That was the choice Pilate gave the crowd two thousand years ago: the popular revolutionary Jesus Barabbas, who would change the world through power, or Jesus of Nazareth, who would change the world through sacrificial love. The crowd shouted,

"Release Barabbas for us!" (Luke 23:18). Had you been standing there that day, whom would you have chosen? (pages 73–75).

• Considering our world today, what kind of messiah would people choose? Whom would you choose? Why?

Bible Study and Discussion

Ask for volunteers to read aloud the following passages of Scripture one at a time. Use the question or suggestion that follows each passage to guide discussion.

ISAIAH 52:13–53:12 (SEE ALSO ISAIAH 42:1-4; 49:1-6; 50:4-9)
• The Gospels seem to suggest that Jesus saw a connection between his suffering and Isaiah's vision of the "suffering servant." And as Adam Hamilton mentions in the book (page 64), the early church also made that connection. Read the fourth Servant Song that begins with Isaiah 52:13 and reflect on how those words support or give meaning to the story of Jesus' suffering.

JOHN 18:28-38
• Compare Jesus' response to Pilate in John's account with Jesus' near silence in the Synoptic accounts.

ACTS 3:11-26 (PETER'S SECOND SERMON); ACTS 8:26-39 (PHILIP AND THE ETHIOPIAN)
• In this sermon, Peter twice uses the term "servant" to refer to Christ and refers to the prophet's prediction that this man would suffer. The Scripture Philip explains to the Ethiopian eunuch is one of the "suffering servant" passages in Isaiah. Why do you think it was so important for the first Christians to acknowledge an Old Testament context for Jesus' suffering and death?

49

Wrapping Up

In Perspective

To conclude the session, ask group members to consider and discuss one or more of the following perspectives. For the painting, print out a color copy and display it or pass it around for the group to see.

IN THE ANTONIA FORTRESS

Imagine yourself next to "the judge's bench at a place called The Stone Pavement" (John 19:13) just outside the fortified home of Pontius Pilate. It is high noon, and the sun is bright and hot. What do you see the Roman guards doing behind you? Look out on the crowds of Jews straining to hear the proceedings. What do you see in their faces? What do you see in Pilate's face? What do you see in Jesus' face? What insights into this part of the Passion story come from reading the faces of those involved in the scene?

INSIDE THE MIND OF BARABBAS

Imagine that you are a criminal, guilty of murder and sedition. You have just been set free because someone you have never met is about to be crucified in your place. What are you thinking? What will you do next?

IN FRONT OF CISERI'S ECCE HOMO

One of the striking characteristics of this painting of Jesus before Pilate is its almost photographic quality. This was one of Antonio Ciseri's trademarks. Notice particularly the perspective of this scene: We view in sharp detail the figures and action from behind. What does the artist want the viewer to know about this moment in the Passion narrative from the way he has painted it? Why do you think he chose to depict the scene from behind? In the painting, whose face is visible and whose is not? Why might that be significant?

Closing Prayer

And after you have suffered for a little while, the God of all grace, who has called you to his eternal glory in Christ, will himself restore, support, strengthen, and establish you. To him be the power forever and ever. Amen. (1 Peter 5:10-11)

Session 5

The Torture and
Humiliation of the King

Getting Started

Session Goals

This session is intended to help participants...
- explore the Gospels' account of Jesus' humiliation at the hands of the Roman soldiers on his way to Calvary;
- explore Jesus' particular experience of suffering as a way of understanding his role in God's redemption of the world;
- consider our own capacity for inhuman acts and attitudes directed toward others and to identify ways to guard against them.

Opening Prayer

I am poured out like water,
    and all my bones are out of joint;
my heart is like wax;
    it is melted within my breast;

my mouth is dried up like a potsherd,
　　and my tongue sticks to my jaws;
you lay me in the dust of death.

For dogs are all around me;
　　a company of evildoers encircles me.
My hands and feet have shriveled;
I can count all my bones.
They stare and gloat over me;
they divide my clothes among themselves,
　　and for my clothing they cast lots.

But you, O LORD, do not be far away!
　　O my help, come quickly to my aid!
Deliver my soul from the sword,
　　my life from the power of the dog!
　　Save me from the mouth of the lion! (Psalm 22:14-21a)

Biblical Foundation

After flogging Jesus, [Pilate] handed him over to be crucified.

Then the soldiers led him into the courtyard of the palace (that is, the governor's headquarters); and they called together the whole cohort. And they clothed him in a purple cloak; and after twisting some thorns into a crown, they put it on him. And they began saluting him, "Hail, King of the Jews!" They struck his head with a reed, spat upon him, and knelt down in homage to him. After mocking him, they stripped him of the purple cloak and put his own clothes on him. Then they led him out to crucify him.

They compelled a passer-by, who was coming in from the country, to carry his cross; it was Simon of Cyrene, the father of Alexander and Rufus. Then they brought Jesus to the place called Golgotha (which means the place of a skull).

And they offered him wine mixed with myrrh; but he did not take it. (Mark 15:15b-23)

Opening Activity

To begin the discussion of Jesus' experience of torture and humiliation, ask the group to cite modern examples of humans being tortured or humiliated. (Possible responses may include Nazi concentration camps, the violence in Darfur, apartheid in South Africa, North Korean labor camps, and the Abu Ghraib prison.) Talk about what motivates human beings to treat their fellow human beings so inhumanely.

Learning Together

Video Presentation and Discussion

Play the video segment for Session 5.
Running Time: 9:06 minutes

SIGHTS
- A whip and whipping post similar to those used by the Romans in the first century AD
- The Chapel of Flagellation and its three stained glass windows depicting Pontius Pilate, Barabbas, and Jesus bound to a Roman column, with a crown of thorns on the ceiling
- The pieces of a Roman cross: the vertical beam (*stipes*) and the horizontal beam (*patibulum*)
- Gordon's Calvary, a skull-shaped rock formation near an unfinished tomb, which was proposed in the late 1800s as the site where Christ was crucified

KEY INSIGHTS
- The Gospels say very little about the flogging of Jesus, and their accounts are slightly different.
- In the beating and humiliation of Jesus, we see evidence of an evil kind of cruelty in which human beings torment one whose very existence is a challenge to them.
- The horizontal beam of the cross Jesus carried weighed nearly 100 pounds. It is likely that after Jesus attempted to carry it some distance, Simon of Cyrene was pressed into service.
- John tells us that Jesus carried his own cross, undoubtedly wanting readers to see the connection to Isaac carrying the wood on which he was about to be sacrificed.

QUESTIONS FOR DISCUSSION
- Why do you think the Gospels say very little about the flogging of Jesus? How do you account for the various placements of the flogging in the four Gospel accounts?
- How do you imagine the scene in which Jesus was mocked? In your mind, how did Jesus respond to this kind of cruelty?
- During the final twenty-four hours of Jesus' life, we see Judas' betrayal, Peter's denial, the disciples' abandonment, the Sanhedrin's jealousy, the crowd's rage, Pilate's acquiescence, and the soldiers' cruelty. What do these sights teach us about what we need saving from?
- What does the example of Simon of Cyrene teach us about discipleship?

Book Study and Discussion

Ask for volunteers to read aloud, one at a time, the following excerpts from Chapter 5 of the book *24 Hours That Changed the World*. Use the questions that follow each excerpt to guide discussion.

In 1963, Stanley Milgram at Yale University invited people to come in off the street to take part in a scientific investigation. They were paid four dollars for one hour in which they were set in front of gauges and dials and told to deliver shocks when someone in the other room gave wrong answers to questions they were asked. The experiment was designed to see how far people would go if an authority figure told them they must go on increasing the force of the shock until it reached apparently fatal levels. No one was actually shocked; but the subjects did not know that, since they could hear but not see the person they supposedly were shocking. Before the experiment, researchers estimated just one percent of the US population would administer what they thought were lethal doses of electricity. What the researchers found was that sixty-five percent of the subjects were willing to increase the electricity to four hundred fifty volts, despite the apparent cries of pain coming from the person in the other room. Even after the cries finally fell silent, the subjects were still willing to give electrical jolts to that person because an authority figure told them they must complete the experiment. Sixty-five percent!...

Ordinary people can be persuaded to do extraordinary and awful things. Given the right combination of ideology, authority, and gradual desensitization, all of us can become monsters, capable of destroying others with weapons ranging from words to gas chambers. It is a reality we must face and guard against, looking instead to God and trying to understand who he has called us to be (page 86).

- What particular Christian practices can help us guard against losing our humanity and supporting actions, attitudes, and policies that we should reject?

The subjective or moral influence theory of the Atonement maintains that the Atonement was not about changing God or making it possible for God to forgive us. It was, rather, about changing you and me. Jesus' suffering, death, and resurrection constitute a divine drama meant to communicate God's Word to humanity, to make clear to us our need for redemption and forgiveness, to show us the full extent of God's love and lead us to repentance. John's Gospel begins with a prologue in which he speaks of Jesus as God's Word. Jesus was God's vehicle for communicating with us, his Word made flesh. In Jesus, God's divine nature was united with human flesh to reveal his character, his love, and his will for humanity (page 89).

- Describe your understanding of the subjective or moral influence theory of the Atonement mentioned in this passage. Does this theory help you make sense of the humiliation, suffering, and death of Jesus? Why, or why not?

There is one more word we should hear in Jesus' suffering and death, and that concerns the nature of sacrificial love. He has set an example for us of a kind of love that alone has the power to save humanity from its self-destructive ways. Sacrificial love transforms enemies into friends, shames the guilty into repentance, and melts hearts of stone. The world is changed by true demonstrations of sacrificial love and by selfless acts of service (page 91).

- What examples of sacrificial love inspire you to greater service in the name of Christ?

Bible Study and Discussion

Ask for volunteers to read aloud the following passages of Scripture one at a time. Use the question that follows each passage to guide discussion.

MARK 15:16
- In this verse, Mark uses "cohort," a term that originally meant one of the ten subdivisions of a Roman legion, several hundred strong. What do you think Mark is trying to emphasize by giving us an image of Jesus surrounded by not just a few, but hundreds of brutal, mocking soldiers?

MATTHEW 2:11 (COMPARE MARK 15:23)
- Myrrh is mentioned twice in the Gospels: once in Matthew's account of Jesus' birth and again in Mark's account of Jesus' crucifixion. What connection do you see between these two offerings?

LUKE 23:26 (COMPARE MATTHEW 27:32 AND MARK 15:21)
- Only Luke mentions that Simon of Cyrene carried Jesus' cross "behind Jesus." What insights into the Passion narrative does that detail provide?

ROMANS 5:6-11
- Why does Paul think it so crucial that Jesus' death proves God's love for us?

Wrapping Up

In Perspective

To conclude the session, ask group members to consider and discuss one or more of the following perspectives. For the painting, print out a color copy and display it or pass it around for the group to see.

ALONG THE VIA DOLOROSA

The path that Jesus traveled from the palace of Pontius Pilate to the cross has come to be called the Via Dolorosa ("the way of suffering"). This path has been, for many centuries, a traditional pilgrimage for Christians. Take that journey in your imagination. Put yourself somewhere in the crowd, trailing the struggling Christ who bears his own crossbeam. What do you see? What do you hear? What do you feel?

INSIDE THE HEART OF SIMON OF CYRENE
Some of the Roman soldiers have just grabbed you from the crowd of people who have been following Jesus. The soldiers force you to your knees. You can see other soldiers approaching you with the crossbeam that Jesus has been carrying. They want you to carry it! At first you struggle to resist, but then . . . what?

IN FRONT OF VERONESE'S JESUS SUCCUMBING TO THE WEIGHT OF THE CROSS
Paolo Veronese is considered to be one of the master colorists of the late Renaissance, meaning that his paintings show the artist's highly imaginative eye for and ability to use colors. He is known for his huge, brightly colored frescoes depicting some of the Bible's familiar feast scenes. However, in this painting of Jesus, his hues are indicative of the mood of his subject. Notice the sky. Contrast the color and actions of the man in the upper right and the women in the lower left. Who acts as the central figure in the painting, the man pictured with his back to the viewer or Jesus on the ground? Why do you think so? What insights into this moment in the story does the painting evoke?

Closing Prayer
Now may our Lord Jesus Christ himself and God our Father, who loved us and through grace gave us eternal comfort and good hope, comfort your hearts and strengthen them in every good work and deed. Amen. (2 Thessalonians 2:16-17)

Session 6

The Crucifixion

Getting Started

Session Goals

- explore the Gospels' account of Jesus' death on the cross;
- compare several ways to think about how Jesus' death saves us;
- hear in Jesus' dying words echoes of his purpose and mission as God's Messiah.

Opening Prayer

My God, my God, why have you forsaken me?
  Why are you so far from helping me, from the words
    of my groaning?
O my God, I cry by day, but you do not answer;
  and by night, but find no rest.

Yet you are holy,
  enthroned on the praises of Israel.

In you our ancestors trusted;
    they trusted, and you delivered them.
To you they cried, and were saved;
    in you they trusted, and were not put to shame.

                                (Psalm 22:1-5)

Biblical Foundation

It was nine o'clock in the morning when they crucified him. The inscription of the charge against him read, "The King of the Jews." And with him they crucified two bandits, one on his right and one on his left. Those who passed by derided him, shaking their heads and saying, "Aha! You who would destroy the temple and build it in three days, save yourself, and come down from the cross!" In the same way the chief priests, along with the scribes, were also mocking him among themselves and saying, "He saved others; he cannot save himself. Let the Messiah, the King of Israel, come down from the cross now, so that we may see and believe." Those who were crucified with him also taunted him.

When it was noon, darkness came over the whole land until three in the afternoon. At three o'clock Jesus cried out with a loud voice, "Eloi, Eloi, lema sabachthani?" which means, "My God, my God, why have you forsaken me?" When some of the bystanders heard it, they said, "Listen, he is calling for Elijah." And someone ran, filled a sponge with sour wine, put it on a stick, and gave it to him to drink, saying, "Wait, let us see whether Elijah will come to take him down." Then Jesus gave a loud cry and breathed his last. And the curtain of the temple was torn in two, from top to bottom. Now when the centurion, who stood facing him, saw that in this way he breathed his last, he said, "Truly this man was God's Son!" (Mark 15:25-39)

Opening Activity

Show the group the illustration used on the next page of this leader guide and on page 97 of the book. This illustration, in which the feet are nailed to the cross in a way most of us have not seen before, is based on archaeological findings of a foot bone of a man who was crucified within decades of Jesus' execution, and probably at Jerusalem.

The foot bone was found in a Jewish cemetery in the northern Jerusalem suburb of Giv'at ha-Mivtar. Clearly visible was the iron spike that pinned the foot to a cross. Remnants of wood were found at the head of the spike, indicating that it had been driven first through a board in order to keep the victim's foot in place. The point of the spike appeared to have been slightly bent, perhaps when it was driven into a knot of the beam.

Discuss the feelings or thoughts that are evoked by this new information about the cruelty of crucifixion.

Learning Together

Video Presentation and Discussion

Play the video segment for Session 6.
Running Time: 12:54 minutes

SIGHTS

- The Church of the Holy Sepulcher, the traditional site considered to encompass both the place where Jesus was crucified and the tomb in which he was buried
- The interior of the Chapel of the Crucifixion and the altar that stands over the Rock of Calvary
- A representation of the cross on which Jesus likely was crucified

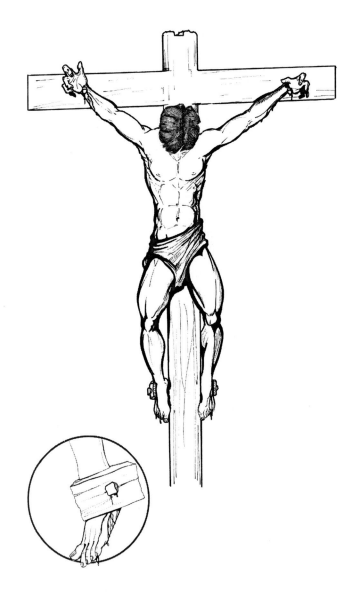

KEY INSIGHTS
- The Orthodox tradition makes elaborate use of icons of brass; they are a reminder of why most Protestants often find these holy sites overwhelming and ostentatious and why they favor Gordon's Cavalry as a place to remember the Crucifixion.
- The cross would have been assembled at the site of the Crucifixion. Archaeological evidence indicates that the victims of crucifixion had their feet nailed into the sides of the cross, straddling it. The small ledge was not for the feet but acted as a seat, encouraging the victim to rest upon it, thus pulling at the nails piercing the wrists. Remember, the aim of crucifixion was to inflict as much pain as possible upon the victim for as long as possible.
- Roman crosses were six to nine feet high. We tend to imagine Jesus hanging high up, but in reality Jesus was likely only a foot or so above those who stood around his cross.

QUESTIONS FOR DISCUSSION
- In his sermon excerpt, Adam says that the cross is a reminder that (1) we need saving, (2) God experiences suffering because of our brokenness, (3) God has chosen to be merciful and forgiving toward us, and (4) God loves us. How do you respond to those reminders?
- What does the cross mean to you?

Book Study and Discussion

Ask for volunteers to read aloud, one at a time, the following excerpts from Chapter 6 of the book *24 Hours That Changed the World*. Use the questions that follow each excerpt to guide discussion.

In the sacrificial offering theory of the Atonement, we view the Crucifixion through the lens of the Old Testament's sacrificial system. In his death, Jesus acted as the high priest representing all of humanity. Throughout the Gospels, Jesus refers to himself as the Son of Man, a title pointing to his role as "representative human being." He was God in the flesh, revealing God to us; but he was also fully human, representing a new humanity that reflected what we were meant to be as human beings. In this capacity, he became our priest and intercessor with God. He offered a sacrifice to God to atone for humanity's sin, to reconcile us with the Father. He offered not a goat or a bull, but himself as the Son of Man and as our high priest. In essence, he said, "Father, for these creatures, so small, so broken, so easily lured into hurting one another, for these men and women who do evil to one another and turn their backs on you—for them I offer myself to you to atone for their sins" (pages 102–103).

- Describe your understanding of the sacrificial offering theory of the Atonement as described in this passage. What aspects of this theory aid or hinder your understanding of the death of Jesus?

Like Psalm 22, nearly all the lament psalms—those that complain because God seems to be nowhere near—end with an affirmation of faith. The very act of praying a complaint psalm is an affirmation of faith. When darkness seems to prevail in your life, it takes faith even to talk to God and complain to him! The last words of Jesus from the cross recorded in the Gospel of Luke reflect Jesus' absolute trust in God: "Father, into your hands I commend my spirit." This is also a model of prayer for all of us when we are afraid, when we are sick, when we face our own death. This prayer says, "I commit myself to you, O God. In my living and in my dying, in the good times and in the bad, whatever I am and have, I place in your hands, O God, for your safekeeping" (page 112).

- When was the last time you complained to God out of an experience of despair or darkness and yet ended up affirming your trust in God? Describe how you moved from lament to trust.

Bible Study and Discussion

Traditionally, Christians have revered the four Gospel accounts of the words Jesus spoke while on the cross. Ask for volunteers to read aloud each of these "seven last words of Christ." After each of the seven sentences, use the following question to guide the group's discussion: How do Jesus' words give meaning to the Gospels' claim of who Jesus is? (See also Adam Hamilton's comments on these passages in Chapter 6 of his book *24 Hours That Changed the World*).

1. "Here is your mother" (John 19:27).

2. "Father, forgive them; for they do not know what they are doing" (Luke 23:34).

3. "Today you will be with me in Paradise" (Luke 23:43).

4. "My God, my God, why have you forsaken me?" (Matthew 27:46; Mark 15:34; see Psalm 22:1).

5. "I am thirsty" (John 19:28).

6. "Father, into your hands I commend my spirit" (Luke 23:46).

7. "It is finished" (John 19:30).

Ask for a volunteer to read aloud Romans 5, focusing especially on verses 6-11. Use the following question to guide discussion.

- According to Romans 5, how does Jesus' death on the cross bring about our salvation?

Wrapping Up

In Perspective

To conclude the session, ask group members to consider and discuss one or more of the following perspectives. For the painting, print out a color copy and display it or pass it around for the group to see.

AT THE FOOT OF THE CROSS

According to Adam Hamilton, it is now believed that most crosses were not much more than nine feet tall. In that case, Jesus would have only been three feet or so above the ground. Imagine that you are standing or sitting just three feet from the spikes that hold Jesus' bloody feet in place on the cross. What image most captivates your attention? What do you hear? How do you respond?

IN THE HEART OF THE ROMAN CENTURION

Imagine that you are standing alone, facing the body of Jesus, now dead upon the cross. You have heard his loud cry and seen him take his last breath. Perhaps you have been nearby since Jesus was nailed to the crossbeam. What is it about Jesus that might have prompted you to say, "Truly this man was God's Son!" (Mark 15:39)?

IN FRONT OF VELÁZQUEZ'S CHRIST ON THE CROSS

One of Velázquez's achievements was to make his paintings seem to come alive with just the right luminosity. The irony in this particular painting is that the dying body of

Christ appears real (or alive) enough to step down from the cross. What other features of Velázquez's Christ strike you? What aspects of the Gospels' account of Christ's death on the cross do you think the painter wanted to portray to his viewers?

Closing Prayer

Grace to you and peace from God our Father and the Lord Jesus Christ, who gave himself for our sins to set us free from the present evil age, according to the will of our God and Father, to whom be the glory forever and ever. Amen.

(Galatians 1:3-5)

Session 7

Christ the Victor

Getting Started

Session Goals

This session is intended to help participants...
- explore the Gospels' account of Jesus' victory over death on Easter morning and of what happened prior to his appearance to the disciples;
- consider the incredible promise of Easter: the hope of life after death;
- examine the *Christus Victor* theory of the Atonement and what it might mean for our lives.

Opening Prayer

O sing to the LORD a new song,
   for he has done marvelous things.
His right hand and his holy arm
   have gotten him victory.
The LORD has made known his victory;
   he has revealed his vindication in
      the sight of the nations.

He has remembered his steadfast love and faithfulness
    to the house of Israel.
All the ends of the earth have seen
    the victory of our God. (Psalm 98:1-3)

Biblical Foundation

When the sabbath was over, Mary Magdalene, and Mary
the mother of James, and Salome bought spices, so that they
might go and anoint him. And very early on the first day of the
week, when the sun had risen, they went to the tomb. They
had been saying to one another, "Who will roll away the stone
for us from the entrance to the tomb?" When they looked up,
they saw that the stone, which was very large, had already
been rolled back. As they entered the tomb, they saw a young
man, dressed in a white robe, sitting on the right side; and
they were alarmed. But he said to them, "Do not be alarmed;
you are looking for Jesus of Nazareth, who was crucified. He
has been raised; he is not here." (Mark 16:1-6)

Opening Activity

In his book *24 Hours That Changed the World,* Adam
Hamilton cites a quotation attributed to Frederick Buechner:
"Resurrection means the worst thing is never the last thing."
Ask group members to reflect on that statement for a moment
and then talk together about what it means to live out that
truth in daily life.

Learning Together

Video Presentation and Discussion

Play the video segment for Session 7.
Running Time: 11:10 minutes

Note to the Leader: This video segment concludes with Adam Hamilton speaking aloud a prayer of thanksgiving and invitation. He asks the group to pray along with him. Be sensitive to those in your group who may find this a powerful invitation to a new or renewed commitment to Christ, and consider talking further about it at a later time.

SIGHTS
- The soft rock used to carve out tombs
- An actual family tomb with its large round stone rolled to the side
- The Stone of Unction in the Church of the Holy Sepulcher, a stone table representing the place where Jesus' body was prepared for burial
- Also in the center of the Church of the Holy Sepulcher, beneath the Rotunda of the Resurrection, a small shrine called an *edicule* which is believed to contain all that remains of the rock tomb of Jesus
- The Garden Tomb, another place believed to have been where Jesus was buried

KEY INSIGHTS
- The practice of using rock burial sites made sense in Palestine because arable land was so scarce and the rock beneath the surface was so soft.
- The rock tomb in Megiddo is one of the few still in existence and clearly shows how difficult it would have been to roll back the stone once it had been set in place.
- The chapel shrine that contains the small piece of stone, encased in glass, believed to be from the tomb of Jesus, is the last Station of the Cross. In contrast, in Red Square, Lenin's preserved body lies encased in glass, nothing more than a figure whose ideas are relics of the past.

73

- Inside the Garden Tomb, you can see that one of the two burial plots is unfinished, leading to speculation that the tomb was never completed after Jesus was resurrected.
- John recounts that Jesus was buried and first seen by Mary Magdalene in that garden, clearly alluding to Jesus' restoration of the original garden of Eden.

QUESTIONS FOR DISCUSSION
- Recall some of the sites you have seen these last few weeks: Gethsemane, the pit beneath Caiaphas' house, the whipping post, the stone pavement, the Stone of Unction, the Garden Tomb. How has seeing these sites and objects informed your understanding of what Jesus means for you? for the world?
- Consider the stark contrast between Lenin's tomb in Moscow (a body encased in glass) and Christ's tomb in the Church of the Holy Sepulcher (a small piece of stone encased in glass). What does that say to you about the human condition and the power of God?
- In John's Gospel, the risen Christ appears in a garden and is mistaken for a gardener. If we are called to participate with Jesus, the Gardener, in restoring and bringing healing to the original garden of our world, what might that look like in your life?

Book Study and Discussion

Ask for volunteers to read aloud, one at a time, the following excerpts from Chapter 7 of the book *24 Hours That Changed the World*. Use the questions that follow each excerpt to guide discussion.

The Easter chronology varies slightly in the four Gospel accounts; but one thing is clear: The idea that Jesus had been raised from the dead was considered unbelievable. In Mark (16:1-8), the women learned Jesus had been raised; but they were filled with terror and were afraid to tell anyone. In Matthew (28:16-17), even after the disciples saw him on the mountain in Galilee, "some doubted." In Luke (24:8-11), Mary and the others told the disciples Jesus had been raised; "but these words seemed to them an idle tale, and they did not believe them." According to Luke (24:12), Peter ran to the tomb; but, while "amazed," it is not clear whether he understood what had happened. In John's account (20:2-9), Peter and John ran to the tomb; but though "they saw the linen wrappings lying there," they still did not understand. Then there is "doubting Thomas," who missed the first resurrection appearance of Jesus to the disciples. Thomas told them, "Unless I see the mark of the nails in his hands, and put my finger in the mark of the nails and my hand in his side, I will not believe" (John 20:25).

How grateful I am for the Gospels and their willingness to record that even the disciples struggled with doubt when it came to the Resurrection (page 122).

- The Gospel writers acknowledged that even those who saw the empty tomb struggled to understand Jesus' resurrection. What part has doubt played in your beliefs about the Resurrection?

The last of the theories of the Atonement we will consider in this book...is often referred to as "Christus Victor"— Christ the Victor. This view...holds that the suffering, death, and resurrection of Christ must be taken together as a powerful word from God announcing God's victory over the powers of evil and over the sin that alienates us from God. They are God's triumph over death, which we, by faith, share....

In Jesus, God entered the boxing arena where evil seems to have the upper hand. He took the worst blows of the enemy, being subject to the powers that conspired to destroy him. He was beaten, abused, and eventually knocked out. But just when the match seemed lost, Jesus arose; and in his resurrection he dealt a finishing blow to the forces of evil, sin, and death. Christ became the Victor. With his victory all humankind was offered the opportunity to join forces with him; to be set free from the power of evil, sin, and death; and to live lives of hope, freedom, and love (pages 126–127).

- What metaphor would you use to describe Christ's victory over sin and death? What meaning could the *Christus Victor* theory of the Atonement have in your life?

Bible Study and Discussion

Ask for volunteers to read aloud the following passages of Scripture one at a time. Use the question that follows each passage to guide discussion.

ACTS 9:1-18
- The Bible describes how Paul himself had an encounter with the resurrected Christ, an encounter that completely transformed him. In what ways would you say your experience with the risen Christ has changed you?

1 CORINTHIANS 15:1-11
- In these verses, Paul powerfully and succinctly proclaims the gospel of Jesus' death and resurrection. Summarize what you understand Paul to be saying and how that message grounds your own faith in Jesus.

1 PETER 3:18-20
- Consider the idea that Jesus sought out those most alienated from God, even in the realm of he dead. How might this idea contribute to your understanding of Jesus' mission in the world?

Wrapping Up

In Perspective

To conclude the session, ask group members to consider and discuss one or more of the following perspectives. For the painting, print out a color copy and display it or pass it around for the group to see.

AT THE TOMB OF THE HOLY SEPULCHER

The Church of the Holy Sepulcher in Jerusalem, known to Eastern Orthodox Christians as the Church of the Resurrection, encompasses both the place where Jesus was crucified and the tomb where he was buried and from which he was raised. Most scholars believe this site (and not the so-called Garden Tomb) is likely to be the place Jesus was crucified and buried. The church's rotunda marks what remains of the place believed to be Jesus' tomb, with the shrine (or *edicule*) containing the Chapel of the Angel. In that room is a piece of rock believed to be part of the stone the angels rolled away from the tomb entrance. Put yourself in front of the stone, now rolled away from where Jesus once lay dead. Touch the stone. Walk inside the cool, dank tomb. Look around. What do you see? What do you smell? What do you hear?

IN THE EYES OF:

Joseph of Arimathea (Mark 15:42-46)

Imagine you are Joseph. You are about to handle the lifeless body of Jesus and transport him to a burial place you own. Not a single one of those who followed Jesus when he was alive is around to help you. What do you see? What do you hear? What do you feel? What are you thinking?

Mary Magdalene (Matthew 28:1-10)

Imagine you are Mary Magdalene. You saw the lifeless body of Jesus and watched Joseph of Arimathea take it away. But now you have arrived at the tomb, and the stone is rolled away from the entrance. Someone is telling you that Jesus is alive. You stumble away in shock. What do you see? hear? feel? What are you thinking?

Cleopas (Luke 24:13-35)

Imagine you are Cleopas. You have been eating with a stranger who seems familiar to you. All of a sudden you know who he is. What do you see? hear? feel? What are you thinking?

Doubting Thomas (John 20:19-29)

Imagine you are Thomas. You have heard your fellow disciples talk about seeing Jesus, but you are not buying it. You will believe it when you see Jesus. Suddenly, there he is! What do you see? hear? feel? What are you thinking?

In Front of Burnand's Disciples Peter and John Rushing to the Sepulcher

In this painting, the Swiss Realism artist Eugene Burnand has captured the moment just after Mary Magdalene has reported to the disciples that Jesus' tomb is empty. Here are Peter and John, looking and leaning forward, like the clouds and the horizon line, toward their destination: the empty tomb. The men's facial expressions and body postures reveal some of their feelings. What story does the artist want us to experience in this scene?

Closing Prayer

"Where, O death, is your victory?
Where, O death, is your sting?"

The sting of death is sin, and the power of sin is the law. But thanks be to God, who gives us the victory through our Lord Jesus Christ. Amen. (1 Corinthians 15:55-57)

Closing Hymn (optional)

To conclude your study of Jesus' last day, consider standing together and singing Isaac Watts' famous hymn, the words of which are printed below. If the words and/or tune are unfamiliar, bring some hymnals for the group to use.

When I survey the wondrous cross
    on which the Prince of Glory died,
my richest gain I count but loss,
    and pour contempt on all my pride.
Forbid it, Lord, that I should boast,
    save in the death of Christ my God;
all the vain things that charm me most,
    I sacrifice them to his blood.

See from his head, his hands, his feet,
    sorrow and love flow mingled down.
Did e'er such love and sorrow meet,
    or thorns compose so rich a crown?

Were the whole realm of nature mine,
    that were a present far too small;
love so amazing, so divine,
    demands my soul, my life, my all.[1]

[1] From "When I Survey the Wondrous Cross," in *The United Methodist Hymnal* (Copyright © 1989 by The United Methodist Publishing House); 298.

CPSIA information can be obtained at www.ICGtesting.com
Printed in the USA
LVOW120847010312

271047LV00001B/4/P